A journal, kept at Nootka Sound, by John R. Jewitt : one of the surviving crew of thee ship Boston, of Boston, John Salter, commander, who was massacred on 22d of March 1803 : interspersed with some account of the natives, their manners and customs.

John Rodgers Jewitt

A

JOURNAL,

KEPT AT

NOOTKA SOUND,

BY

JOHN R. JEWITT.

ONE OF THE SURVIVING CREW OF THE SHIP BOSTON, OF
BOSTON, JOHN SALTER, COMMANDER, WHO WAS
MASSACRED ON 22D OF MARCH, 1803.

INTERSPERSED WITH SOME ACCOUNT OF THE

NATIVES, THEIR MANNERS AND CUSTOMS.

∿∿∿∿∿∿

BOSTON: PRINTED FOR THE AUTHOR.

1807.

A

JOURNAL.

WE arrived at Nootka Sound the 12th of March, 1803, all in good health, and anchored five miles above the village in twenty-five fathoms water, muddy bottom. On the 13th the natives visited us and brought a plenty of fresh salmon, which we purchased for fish hooks, &c.; on the 14th our people were on shore getting wood and water for the ship. The natives visited us with a number of canoes round the ship. On the 15th Maquina, the chief, came on board to dine with the captain. After dinner the captain made him a present of a double barrel musket, with which he was much delighted and went on shore. Our people were employed as usual until the 19th when the chief came on board with nine pair of ducks as a present to the captain, and told him that the double barrel musket was not a good one, and that he had broken the lock; captain Salter was very angry, called him a liar, took the musket and threw it down into the cabin and called for me to know whether I could repair it, I told him it could be done. The chief returned to the shore very angry and the captain took no more notice of what had happened. On the 22d the chief came again on board, looked much pleased, had a mask over his face and a whistle in his hand, seemed to be very happy and asked the captain when he should go to sea; "Tomorrow," replied the captain, "Why don't you go to Friendly cove and fish, there is a plenty of salmon there," said the chief. The captain spoke to Mr. Deliewser, and they agreed it would be a very good plan to get a stock of fresh salmon to carry to sea. After dinner the captain dispatched the jolly boat with Mr. Deliewser and nine of the people. The steward was on shore washing the captain's cloaths; the sail maker was in the main hatches at work upon the sails; I was in the steerage cleaning muskets. About one hour after the boat was gone, the captain told Mr. Ingraham to hoist in the long boat, saying there was a sufficient number of the natives on board to help to pull at the tackle falls to hoist her in. When they had got the boat half way up, the natives seized every man at his tackle fall, and likewise the Captain, threw him over the quarter deck, and killed every man with his own knife taken out of his pocket, and cut off their heads and threw their bodies overboard. Hearing a noise on deck, I went and got my musket, and ascending the stairs was caught by the hair of the head, by three of the natives. One of them struck at me with an axe and cut my forehead, but having short hair, their hands slipt and I fell down the steerage. The Chief, observing it was me, told them all not to hurt me, for that I was an armourer and would be of great service to him. He ordered his people to shut over the hatch. I lay in a most deplorable state; being very weak in consequence of the loss of blood from the cut I received. After they had taken the ship they sent canoes off to murder the men that were in the boat, which they soon did and brought their heads, which amounted to twenty-five, on board, and placed them in a right line on the quarter deck. I remained below four hours, when the Chief called me on deck and told me that I must be his slave and work for him and he would spare my life, to which I of course assented. The Chief led me on the quarter deck and told me to look at all the people's heads that were placed in a line, at which sight the reader can better imagine what were my feelings than I can describe them. It was about 5 o'clock, P. M. the Chief told me I must get the ship under way and take her into the Cove, where we arrived at 8 o'clock in the evening. The Chief then took me ashore, and I slept at his house. As soon as I arrived in the house the natives came around me and seemed to sympathize in my captivity. I was very uneasy and in a great deal of pain. I laid myself down to go to sleep, but was alarmed about 12 o'clock by one of the natives coming into the house, who told me that there was one of our people still alive. I was rejoiced to hear the news, reflecting that I should be much more happy for having a partner in exile. I immediately went on board and to my great joy found it to be our Sailmaker, Thompson : he had received a stab in the nose. The Chief expressed great satisfaction in his being saved, saying he would be very useful to make sails for his canoes. On the 24th, several of the natives were employed in getting the powder and muskets, cloth, &c. out of the ship, others cutting the sails from the yards, and the masts down, making her a complete wreck so that it should be impossible for her to proceed again to sea.

March 25.—This day arrived two ships, one as we suppos-
ed was about three hundred tons with yellow sides, and a fig-
ure head, but no top gallant masts up, and the other built after
the manner of the French corvettes with red sides. The natives being so well provided for them by the ammunition of
which they had plundered us, fired on them so briskly that
they were thrown into great consternation, but the ships were
so far out in the bay, that it was impossible to reach them,
the natives ashore having only muskets and blunderbusses.
The ships fired grape shot but to no effect. They about ship
and went to sea. Our Chief soon regretted having fired upon
them, for he feared that they would inform other vessels and
prevent them from coming to trade with him. A few
days after other tribes of natives not less than twenty in number came from the northward and southward.

On their coming into the harbour Maquina's tribe ran
down upon the beach, and he and I went upon the house top ;
we were employed in drumming. Thompson was stationed
at the great guns which had been taken from our ship. He
gives the word of command fire, but they are not like the
Europeans, for most of them are afraid to fire even a musket.
It was curious to see them kneeling down with the butt end
of their muskets on the ground ; their dress and appearance
so singular too—some with eight muskets on their shoulders—
some with eight powder horns, and stockings round their
necks, running up and down the beach in the greatest consternation. Maquina invites them into his house and provisions are prepared for them, such as whale's blubber, raw herring spawn, and cold water, of which they appear to make a
hearty feast. After the repast is over, they are ordered out
of the house in order that preparation may be made for the
dance which soon succeeded, and when our Chief exhibited
his child with a masque on his face drest in a most curious
manner.

After the dance our Chief begins to give presents to the
strangers. I saw him give one hundred muskets, four hundred yards of cloth, one hundred looking glasses, twenty barrels of powder, &c.

March 28 —Maquina would not permit the strangers to
sleep in his house, but in their canoes on the beach. My
partner and myself were ordered with a brace of pistols to
keep watch all night over the ship's cargo. Other tribes of
Indians come every day to trade with our Chief, bringing

with them whale's blubber, train oil, dried clams, herrings, &c. and receiving in return cloth, &c.

March 29.—Last night one of the natives having gone on board the ship with a lighted fire-brand in his hand with an intention to steal, dropt a spark of fire down in the hold. The ship immediately caught fire, and was entirely consumed, a great part of the cargo and all the ship's provisions were destroyed, which latter loss we regretted the more as we should have had the ship's provisions entirely to ourselves, the natives not eating any of them.

30. The natives regret the loss of the ship; we are still keeping watch night and day. As we were looking over the remaining part of the ship's cargo we found a box of chocolate, which much delighted us; having had for some time nothing to eat but whale's blubber and train oil, which can be easily conceived by civilized people not to have been very delicious to our tastes or our stomachs. Natives coming as usual, bringing skins, provision, slaves, &c. I was in great hopes that I might have been sold, so that I might have been able to have sent letters to masters of ships informing them that we were alive, so that they might come and release us from the slavery of savages who had stript us of our clothes and our provisions, and literally made us hewers of wood and drawers of water.

June 1. (Wednesday.) Employed ourselves cutting firewood. Our Chief out whaling. Fresh breezes from the N. W. Our Chief returned without success.

2. This day my partner and myself invited to a feast at another Chief's house. When we sat down they put before us two large pieces of porpoise, but being very hungry we ate considerable, and what was left we were obliged to carry home with us.

3. Fine and clear weather. A. M. Was invited to a feast consisting of dried clams and train oil. P. M. Employed cutting fire-wood.

4. Weather fine and clear. Went about a mile to wash our cloaths. Fresh breezes from N. W.

5. Invited to a feast consisting of boiled salmon which was a feast indeed to us. Their mode of cooking salmon is very curious. They have a large wooden vessel, which they fill with water which they heat by putting red hot stones into it. When the water boils they put in the salmon, and keep the water hot by the constant application of the heated stones.

When the salmon is in this way sufficiently boiled, they put it into a wooden dish and eat it with their fingers.

Monday 6. Pleasant weather, natives fishing; our chief out whaling, P. M. returned without success. Chief invited to a feast of herring spawn.

7. Thompson employed making trowsers for himself and and me. I was employ'd in cleaning muskets for our chief.

8. Foggy weather with heavy rains, employed as usual.

9. Fine weather. Walked from house to house begging for something to eat, we went into house and they asked us to eat cockles, we accepted the offer, thanked them, and returned home.

10. Clear weather, employed ourselves mending the long boat.

11. The girls that belonged to our chief went to gather bramble berries; returned in the afternoon with three bushels.

12. Washed ourselves, put on clean shirts, &c. went out amongst the bushes with a prayer book, to pray to God to send a ship to release us.

13. Our chief out whaling, returned without success. Employed cleaning muskets.

14. Employed as usual. Thompson making a sail for our chief's canoe. Invited to eat whale's blubber.

15. Cloudy weather. Thompson employed making sails for canoes, I was cleaning muskets, our chief out whaling.

16. A.M. employed cutting fire wood. P.M. invited to a feast consisting of dried clams and train oil. Our chief returned from fishing, having had no success was in bad humour.

17. Pleasant weather; employed cleaning muskets.

18. Washed our cloaths. Had nothing to eat all day.

19. Invited to a feast of seal's blubber.

20. Our girls belonging to the chief went to gather bramble berries. Chief out whaling.

21. The chief out whaling. I was employed in cleaning muskets. Thompson making trowsers. Afternoon our girls returned with four bushels of bramble berries, which our chief divided among his people. We used to always go shares amongst them.

22. Our chief out whaling, struck one and was near to him one day and one night, and then his line parted. Returned and was very cross.

23. Employed cutting fire wood.

24. Invited to a feast consisting of train oil and dried clams.

25. Pleasant weather. Employed washing, &c. Afternoon returned home—was invited to a feast.

26. Fine clear weather. I happened to see one of the natives with an almanack, which I bought of him for a knife and found it very useful.

27. Cloudy weather. Employed cleaning muskets.

38. Our chief out whaling. Fresh breezes from the Eastward. Afternoon—returned without success.

29. Clear weather. Invited to eat blubber, but refused to go.

30. Pleasant weather. This day I took a walk out in the woods, sat down and was reading a book when our chief came and asked me if I were hungry ; I told him yes ; I went home and he ordered me some herring spawn.

July 1. Our chief out whaling. We were invited to a feast of dog fish. Afternoon our chief returned without success.

2. Foggy weather. Employed repairing the jolly boat.

3. Employed cutting fire wood. Afternoon, saw a ship standing to the northward, about 9 leagues from Nootka.

4. Our chief out whaling—no success.

5. Clear weather. Employed cutting fire wood. Invited to a feast consisting of raw herring spawn and cold water.

6. Employed cleaning muskets, &c. Considerable thunder and lightning which frighten the natives very much.

7. We have had nothing to eat for two days but nettle stalks which we gathered in the fields ; our chief gave us this day a piece of blubber, which to us, hungry as we were, was very delicious.

9. One of the natives took Thompson along with him, to shew him some turnips and some onions which the Spaniards had planted. We gathered some and had them boiled.

10. Pleasant weather. Employed cleaning muskets. Invited to a feast consisting of cockles.

11. Our chief out whaling ; returned without success.

12. Invited to a feast of whale's blubber.

13. Our chief out fishing ; employed cleaning muskets. P. M. Our chief returned with twenty salmon.

14. Employed cutting fire wood ; Thompson making a garment for our chief. P. M. Invited to eat raw herring spawn.

15. Pleasant weather. Our chief gave to us four yards of canvass, of which Thompson made trowsers, &c.

16. Pleasant weather ; employed washing our clothes ; natives fishing.

17. Clear weather; natives fishing; invited to eat seal's blubber.

18. Our chief out whaling; Returned, no success; these are very hungry times with us; for when the chief is out whaling and all his people with him we get nothing to eat, and he will not let us go a fishing with him for fear we should go away to another tribe.

19. Foggy weather; natives fishing; returned with plenty of cod fish.

August 18. (Thursday.) Our days have passed away without any unusual occurrence. This day a canoe arrived from the Cla-u-quate and informed us that there was a ship laying at anchor at the Cheenooks; they told us that the captain had a wooden leg, and that he was afraid to come to Nootka, he having heard of our ship's being cut off.

20. Clear weather; employed washing our shirts.

21. Fine weather; took a walk in the woods with a prayer er book, and prayed most earnestly that a ship might come to our release.

September 3. (Saturday.) A. M. Left Nootka to go to Tashes, which is about 30 miles up the sound. We having a fair wind arrived there P. M. 4 o'clock. The natives made themselves huts of some spars. They leave Nootka every year and go to Tashes to get their winter stock of provisions.

4. Rainy weather. This day (Sunday) washed ourselves and went to prayers.

20. The natives fishing with little success; but told us next month they would go home with their canoes full. This day our chief told me, that if ever he caught me writing my journal any more he would burn it, for he said I was writing bad about him. Notwithstanding his threats I shall continue to avail myself of every opportunity to fill it up when he is fishing.

30. A canoe arrived; informed us that the same captain with a wooden leg was still laying at the Cheenooks; I asked the natives, if he knew of Thompson and myself being ashore at Nootka. They told me he did. I sent a letter by one of the natives unknown to our chief to the king of Wickeningish. When the natives returned they told me they had delivered the letter to the king, and he said he would give it to the first ship that arrived.

October 10. (Monday.) I went with our chief a fishing. It was very curious to see them strike the salmon with a small rod eighteen feet long with a piece of sharp bone at the end of it. Came home with thirty salmon.

20   Went a fishing with our chief. He had a large scene set in a fortunate place, for it had not been down ten minutes before it was full with seven hundred salmon, which we brought home in our canoe. The women are employed in cutting and drying them.

21. Heavy rains, with the wind S. E.

22. Thompson employed making a garment out of waistcoat pieces for our chief; when finished he was perfectly satisfied and thought it very elegant.

23. Natives fishing. We had plenty of salmon to eat, having caught them in great numbers.

24. Our chief informed me, that not long ago there were six men ran away in the night, on account of bad treatment from the captain, and for being kept on short allowance, from the ship Manchester, of Philadelphia, at the time when she lay at Nootka. He gave me a book belonging to one of the men that had ran away, named Daniel Smith, and I found by looking into it, that the other men's names were Lewis Gillion, James, Toms, Benjamin Johnson, Jack Clark. In this book I found the following entries: "Bristol, Sept. 8, 1800, shipped on board the ship Manchester, Capt. Bria. On Monday 8th, received our notes; on Saturday 14th, do. Left port on Sunday, Oct. 19." I was informed by our chief that six of them went away in the night unknown to him, expecting to get to the Wickenishes, but being very hungry, they were obliged to stop at the Esquates, several miles this side of their intended port. The natives stopt them from going any further, knowing they belonged to our chief, and brought them back to Nootka. He was very angry, ordered them to be killed, which the natives did. The boy Jack did not run away, so his life was spared, and sold to the Wickenishes. Soon after we arrived he heard of our ship's being cut off. He died in May, 1803.

25. The weather being very bad, the natives could not go a fishing. Thompson employed making a garment for our chief.

26. Rainy weather; natives fishing; employed making fish hooks out of nails.

27. Invited to a feast consisting of fresh herrings. Heavy rains; natives returned with a plenty of salmon.

28. Weather stormy; thunder and lightning.

29. Clear weather; invited to eat fresh salmon; employed as usual.

30. Frosty and clear weather with snow on the mountains. Went with our chief a fishing; returned with seven hundred salmon, of which the Tashees abound. There were brought to our chief's house to day twenty-five hundred.

31. Foggy weather with rain. Arrived a canoe with six natives, from a small village called Newchadlate, with ifraw, which is like white beads, to put round their necks, it is called very valuable.

November 1. (Tuesday.) This month comes in with heavy rains and winds variable. Arrived a canoe from the Wickeningish. Our chief was informed that they had been at war with another tribe called Ah-char-arts, and killed men and women to the amount of one hundred and fifty. They brought to our chief nine slaves as a present. He gave them in return cloth, muskets, powder, shot, &c.

2. Cloudy weather. Invited to a feast consisting of train oil and dried fish. Our chief has nine wives, all employed cutting the salmon to dry.

3. Clear and frosty; employed washing our shirts &c.; invited to eat seal's blubber; natives fishing.

4. Went with our chief a fishing; returned with two hundred salmon. P. M. I went a shooting, returned with five pair of ducks which we had cooked for supper.

5. Frosty weather. Our chief went to haul the scene; returned with fifty salmon. Invited to eat dried muscles and train oil.

6. Our chief's wife and her attendants went to gather bramble berries; the chief went to walk upon a high mountain, singing all the day for whales to come that he might kill them.

7. Our chief's wife returned with two bushels of berries.

8. Frosty and clear with snow on the mountains; natives fishing.

9. Heavy rains last night. Our chief went a fishing; I was employed cleaning muskets for another chief, which having done he always gave me something to eat.

10. The weather foggy. Natives fishing. Arrived a canoe from the Aitizarts with four skins for our chief.

11. Frosty weather. Employed making copper rings out of nails to go round the wrist, polished for an ornament

12. Rainy weather. Natives fishing. Invited to eat blubber.

13. Thick and cloudy. Arrived a canoe from Savahina with fresh herrings a present to our chief. This being Sunday went to prayers as usual.

14. Frosty weather. Employed as usual. Invited to eat salmon spawn, after that whale's blubber.

15. Fine and clear. Our chief's wife out gathering bramble berries. Arrived a canoe with six natives from Aitizarts with ifraw for our chief; he gave in return cloth, &c.

16. Frosty weather. Natives fishing. Arrived a canoe from Chewmadart with a large chest of salmon spawn for our chief.

17. Invited to eat dried salmon and train oil.

18. Natives Fishing. Our chief's wife returned.

19. Rainy weather. Invited to eat sea cow's blubber. Arrived a canoe from Aitizarts with ifraw for our chief.

20. Natives fishing. Arrived a canoe from Aitizarts with ifraw for our chief.

21. Fine and clear weather. Our chief went to a small village; returned with two baskets of dried salmon.

22. Frosty weather. Invited to eat dried clams and train oil.

23. Arrived a canoe from Esquates with six hundred weight of blubber, being taken from a whale that had been driven ashore in a gale of wind.

24. Rainy weather. Arrived four canoes, one from Savahina, and three from Aitizarts. Our chief had a large feast and a dance; after the dance was over the chief gave away to the amount, muskets two hundred, two hundred yards of cloth, one hundred chemises, one hundred looking glasses, and seven barrels of powder.

25. Fine and clear. Natives fishing, &c.; plenty of fresh herrings.

26. Frosty weather. I was out fishing for herrings; returned with a canoe full.

27. Rainy weather. This being Sunday went to prayers.

28. Clear weather. Invited to eat whale's blubber. Natives fishing. Arrived a canoe from Ah-ow-zerts with skins.

29. Clear weather. This day our chief informed us that he was going to war with the natives of Columbia's Cove, and that I must make some daggers out of old bolts. I went to work with my fire made of green wood, without any bellows, and a large stone for my anvil.

30. Employed making daggers; finished one which much pleased our chief.

December 1. (Thursday.) This month generally comes in with rainy weather. One of the natives caught a large bear, for which he set a snare near a run of fresh water. As soon as they brought him into the house they garnished him with white feathers, and put before him a tray full of train oil.

2. Thompson employed in making an axletree for a grindstone for me to polish my daggers with. Afternoon, was invited to eat fresh salmon.

3. Employed as usual. Natives fishing. Our chief in good humour, because I was making daggers that pleased him.

4. Employed as usual. Afternoon, washed ourselves, &c.

5. Rainy weather. This day I was told that there were only seven of the natives who had eaten of the bear. It was a custom amongst them that whenever any one eats of a wild beast that he must not for two months afterwards eat fresh salmon, fresh herrings, nor any fresh fish out of the sea.

6. This day Maquina gave me much information on the causes of the destruction that had befallen our ship's crew.—One capt. Tawnington, in a schooner, which had wintered in Friendly Cove went on shore with fourteen of his people.—Knowing that Maquina and several of the natives had gone to the Wickeninishes to purchase a wife, he went into his house where were several of the natives' wives, put them into great terror, and plundered our chief of forty skins—immediately returned to his vessel, weighed anchor and went away. Soon after this a capt. Hannah much offended the natives. One of them had been on board his ship, and stole from him a carpenter's chissel. The next day there being a number of canoes lying along side the ship the captain fired upon them and killed men, women and children to the number of twenty. The chief being on board jumped from the quarter deck and swam ashore. A little time before, the Spanish had brutally killed three of their chiefs. They were therefore resolved to have revenge on the first ship they should fall in with, which unfortunate event happened to befal us.

7. This day our chief went to the Ai-tiz-arts, he had an invitation two days before.

8. Frosty weather. The natives caught another wild bear.

9. Rainy weather. Invited to a feast of seal's blubber.

10. Very severe thunder and lightening which much terrified the natives.

11. Natives fishing, &c. Afternoon invited to eat clams and train oil.

12. Frosty weather. Employed as usual.

13. This day our chief began a most curious farce. When all the chiefs were invited to a feast; all of a sudden, the chief fired a pistol off close against his son's ear, which frightened them all. The natives running up and down the village, pulling their hair out from their heads by handfulls, crying out our chief's son is dead. All of a sudden came into the house two men dressed in wolves' skins and took the child away on their backs. We were ordered out of the house, for seven days, and if we came within that time he said he would kill us. After the seven days had expired he called for us to come to the house.

21. This day the farce ended with a horrible sight. Three of the natives were pierced through the flesh of each side near to the ribs with a bayonet. This play is performed every year in the month of December, and is their mode of celebrating the praises of their God and rendering him thanks for all his blessings for the past year.

22. Natives employed fishing. I was employed in making daggers.

23. Rainy weather. Invited to eat whale's blubber. Afternoon—natives fishing. Employed making daggers.

24. Employed in making daggers of a different form; they are made eighteen inches long, and polished so as to see one's face in them.

25. This being Christmas day, we bought our suppers, consisting of dried clams and train oil. Employed as usual.

26. Arrived a canoe from Ai-tiz-arts with train oil for our chief. Bought a dagger of me for which I received two fathoms of cloth and one coat.

27. I was employed in making a dagger for another chief.

28. Employed as usual. Thompson washing our clothing.

29. Frosty weather. Natives fishing.

30. Clear weather. Thompson making a coat for our chief.

31. This morning we left Tasshees to go to Cooptee, which is sixteen miles down the sound, where we arrived at 2 o'clock, P. M.

January 1, 1804. (Sunday.) The new year comes in with snow which is the first we have had this season. Invited to eat dried salmon and train oil.

2. Natives employed in making their houses. Thompson and myself employed as usual.

3. Frosty weather. Natives fishing, &c.

4 Invited to eat whale's blubber. At 6 o'clock, P. M. our chief went a fishing.

5. Finished our chief's dagger ; he made me a present of two quarts of powder.

6. Last night a woman was delivered of a child ; this morning I saw her setting by a fire roasting herring and singing a song.

7. This morning I went with our chief to another nation, I was invited to stop two days at the Ai-tiz-arts which is about thirty miles up the sound. As soon as we arrived the natives came down upon the beach and fired their musquets, receiving us with these words *wharcash, wharcash,* that is, very good.

8. This morning the natives began a tragedy which appeared very terrible to the eye. Twenty men with two arrows each run through the flesh close to their ribs and through their arms, having two men with strings made fast to the arrows that were through the flesh and pulling back as hard as they could. After the play we returned home, arrived at Cooptee at 12 o'clock at night.

9. We get plenty to eat at this place, numbers of herring, salmon, small fish, &c. were caught.

10. A canoe arrived from the Ai-tiz-arts with 600 weight of blubber which was taken from a whale that had died at sea and was driven a shore by a gale of wind. At night our chief bought my dagger for which he gave me a coat that was made and another one that was not finished.

11. Arrived a canoe from Esquates with our chief's daughter ; her husband had been beating her and she came to complain of it to her father. It was thought a war would be the consequence.

12. Natives fishing. Employed as usual.

13. This morning the young chief that had been four months with us went home. He belonged to the Wickeninishes.

14. Was invited to eat fresh salmon. We finished ten daggers for our chief, which pleased him very much.

15. This day there was a grand feast at our chief's house. One of the natives had 5 quarts of salmon spawn boiled and four quarts of train oil mixt together, four dried salmon to eat, but before he began he drank three points of oil ; while he was eating our chief gave him three musquets and one fathom of cloth. He eat till he puked in the dish and then gave over.

16. Our chief sent a canoe with ten natives to the Wick-eninishes to invite them to come and eat with him.

17. Invited to eat fresh salmon.

18. Natives fishing—employed as usual.

19. I was employed in making a dagger for Thompson.

20. Employed as usual in making a dagger for a chief.

21. Natives fishing. Afternoon—Returned with plenty of herring. Invited to eat some.

22. Finished Thompson's dagger. Invited to a feast consisting of seal's blubber and dog fish.

23. Arrived a canoe from Moowachart with dried salmon for our chief.

24. This day our chief had a dance at his house by his son; after the dance he invited the whole village to eat fresh salmon. There were one hundred and twenty large salmon boiled in one tub.

25. Employed in engraving the daggers.

26. This day I finished engraving one of the daggers, with which the chief was much pleased. My engraving tools were made of pieces of old files.

27. Finished engraving a dagger for Thompson which he sold for a coat and one fathom of cloth.

28. A heavy gale of wind which took the planks from the tops of the houses—Natives employed in securing them.

29. Arrived a canoe from Ai-tiz-arts with ifraw for our chief.

30. Employed cleaning musquets; Thompson made a sail for a canoe.

31. Made three daggers for myself and one for Thompson.

February 1. (Wednesday) This day we were obliged to give our chief a great coat and one fathom of cloth to keep in his favour. We understood that if no ships arrived next Spring, he meant to make us go naked like the natives.

2. Clear weather. Natives fishing. Employed cutting fire wood.

3. Employed cutting fire wood. P. M. Returned; invited to eat blubber.

4. Natives fishing. Employed cutting fire wood.

5. Rainy weather. Arrived a canoe from Ai-tiz-arts with three slaves for our chief, he gave in return for them powder, shot, &c.

6. This evening our chief's wife was delivered of a fine boy.

7. Clear weather. Plenty of herrings caught by the natives.

8. This day arrived ten canoes from Ai-tiz-arts, with an hundred natives to eat at the feast of our chief, who made them a present of muskets, coats, cloth, &c.

9. Employed making fish hooks. Natives fishing, &c.

10. Arrived four canoes from Caruquates; the chief of this tribe came with an intention to buy me, but our chief was not willing to part with me.

11. Invited to eat cockles. P. M. Went to cut fire wood.

12. Rainy weather. Employed cutting fire wood; P. M. returned. Our chief gave us some dried salmon and train oil.

13. Frosty weather. Natives fishing. Arrived twenty canoes from the Michlate with salmon spawn for our chief.

14. I have been sick these last four days, owing to the provisions I was obliged to eat.

15. Fine and clear weather. This day finished three daggers for myself.

16. Employed making Thompson a dagger. Invited to eat fresh salmon.

17. Rainy weather. Finished Thompson's dagger.

18. Employed washing our clothing. Invited to eat blubber.

19. (Sunday,) Clear weather. Went to prayers as usual.

20. Invited to eat dried hallibut and train oil.

21. Employed washing our clothes. Arrived a canoe from the northward, to inform our chief there were twenty-ships coming to Nootka in order to destroy his tribe, which caused him to look very shy upon us.

22. We now began to be down-hearted, for our chief said he would cut off another ship if he possibly could; but I hope God will prevent him.

23. Rainy weather. This day the strangers went away. All the natives discourse of is to cut off another ship if one arrives.

24. Arrived a canoe from the same tribe with eight natives, who brought the same news respecting the ships, which frightened us very much.

25. Frosty weather. This day we left Cooptee to return to Nootka, which is about twenty miles distance, having been there almost two months; arrived at Nootka, 4 o'clock, P. M. having had hard work and nothing to eat.

26. Employed making our houses. Arrived two canoes from the Wickeninishes. Went to prayers as usual.

27. Fine and clear. We entertained hopes of seeing a ship in the course of two month's time.

28. Natives fishing.

March 1. (Wednesday.) Clear weather. Saw twelve whales out in the offing.

2. This day our chief-had a feast at his house ; ninety salmon were cooked in one tub. P. M. The strangers went away.

3. Natives fishing, &c. Employed cutting fire wood.

4. Rainy weather. Saw a great number of wild ducks and geese.

5. Invited to eat whale's blubber. P. M. Employed making a dagger by order of the chief.

6. Rainy weather. This day one of the natives was drowned while he was fishing, the wind came on to blow so hard that his canoe upset.

7. Clear weather. Employed cutting fire wood.

8. Arrived a canoe with forty fresh salmon for our chief.

9. Employed washing our clothing ; P. M. returned. Invited to eat seal's blubber.

10. Clear weather. Natives fishing, &c.

11. This day one of the chiefs bought the daughter of another for a wife. One of the natives ran through a large fire naked, for which he received four muskets and five fathoms of cloth.

12. This day the Wickeninishes left us. Employed cutting fire wood.

13. Employed washing our clothes. Gave our chief a coat and one fathom of cloth, which I had received of another chief for a dagger.

14. Rainy weather. Employed mending our clothes. Invited to a feast of whale's blubber.

15. This day the natives fishing ; returned with plenty of salmon ; informed us they saw a ship going to the southward.

16. Clear weather. Employed making fish hooks out of nails.

17. Rainy weather. Natives fishing, &c. Invited to eat seal's blubber. Arrived a canoe from Ai-tiz-arts with ifraw for our chief.

18. Blows a heavy gale of wind from the S. E. which is the severest we have experienced since coming on shore ; I make no doubt of there being very heavy gales in the winter, but being at Tasshes, thirty miles in the country, did not experience them.

19. The gales abated. Natives fishing. Went to prayers.

20. This day a child of our chief's sister died, a boy about eleven years of age. In the night after his death, our chief with eighty men and women began to cry so loud that Thompson and myself were very much frightened, so much so, that we got up and left the house. In the morning our chief made a large feast and burnt ten fathoms of cloth, and buried with the boy eighty fathoms of ifraw, ten fathoms of cloth, and four fine skins. It is the custom when a chief dies to bury all his skins, and whatever other property he is worth, with him.

21. This day I measured one of the natives of about thirty years of age, he was three feet three inches high.

22. We begin to look for ships every day, hoping for our release as soon as one shall arrive. Our sufferings amongst these savages are incredible, for they are the most filthy people in the world, eating the vermin of their own bodies while cooking their meals. We are very much disheartened.

23. Employed washing our clothing. Invited to a feast.

24. Fine and clear weather. Natives fishing, &c.

25. Employed cutting fire wood.

26. The weather thick and cloudy with rain. Invited to a feast.

27. Clear weather. Natives fishing; returned with plenty of cod.

28. Arrived a canoe from Ai-tiz-arts; our chief was informed of an accident that lately happened there. One of the people was trying a musket which he did not observe was loaded, it went off and killed two of his own children and wounded three others. P. M. They went away.

29. Employed cleaning muskets.

30. Rainy weather. Natives fishing. Employed cutting fire wood.

31. Employed making a tent of No. 1 canvass for our chief to set in to look out for whales. Our provisions at this time consist of raw herring spawn and cold water, which we are obliged to eat.

April 1. (Saturday.) Rainy weather. Last night one of our chief's children died; it was three months old. All the natives in the village during the night made a most terrible noise. In the morning he had a dance in his house, after which he distributed among the natives three barrels of gunpowder to sport with.

2. (Sunday.) Clear weather. Natives fishing, &c. Afternoon went to prayers as usual.

3. Rainy weather. Employed cutting fire wood.

4. Clear weather. Natives fishing ; little success.

5. This day our chief went out a whaling, it being the first time this season. In the afternoon he returned ; no success.

6. Thick and cloudy weather. Our chief out whaling ; struck one and was fast, but his harpoon broke and he lost him : returned very cross.

7. Fine and clear weather. Natives fishing, with no success. Our provisions as well as the natives' consist of cockles and muscles, the winter stock of provisions being all expended.

8. Cloudy weather. This day there were ten canoes out whaling, they struck five whales, but their harpoons drawed, and they returned without having caught any.

9. Rainy weather. The times are now very hard with us, for we cannot get any thing to eat except what we are obliged to sell our wearing apparel for. The natives eat only once a day, and their meal consists of cockles, muscles, &c. Thank God, we have been very healthful during the last thirteen months. But now we begin to have a very heavy flux upon us, which is owing to the provisions we are forced to eat. Went to prayers for our release.

10. Our chief out whaling ; returned, no success.

11. Last night our chief informed me he was concerned for his life, because there were no fish to be caught ; he told me that his own people were going to kill him, and he ordered me to keep watch over him night and day with a brace of pistols and a cutlass.

12. Thick weather, with rain. Our chief out a whaling ; returned with no success. Employed as usual keeping watch.

13. Clear weather. Our chief out whaling, struck one but his harpoon drawed, which caused him to lose the whale, and he returned very angry.

14. Thick weather. Our chief's harpoon was made of a very large muscle shell, but so thin that as soon as he struck a whale the shell broke. I told him I could make him a very good one out of steel, and it should be as sharp as a knife ; he ordered me to go to work upon it immediately, which I did, and fixed it for him.

15. Our chief employed trying his new harpoon, which he thinks will answer very well ; he was very much pleased with me for it, and said if he killed a whale he would give me plenty to eat.

16. Fine and clear weather. Our chief out whaling. Hard times with us; eat only once a day; no fish can be caught by the natives, they are afraid there will be a famine amongst them. About two o'clock, P. M. our chief struck a whale and killed him, about five o'clock he was towed by forty canoes, into the cove. The chief was very much delighted with the harpoon I had made for him.

17. This day one of the natives struck a whale and killed it, and gave to our chief six hundred weight of blubber.

18. Employed at cutting up our chief's whale. The natives have now a great plenty, they eat twenty times in the course of the day. Our chief gave me an hundred weight of blubber, and told me I might cook it as I pleased, and I used to boil a piece of it with some young nettles which served for greens.

19. This day employed making lances for our chief eighteen inches long to lance whales; he had never used any before, but he liked the form of them, and said he knew they would answer and was very well pleased with them. Nothing to eat but whale's blubber.

20. Fine and clear. This day finished two lances made out of a flat bar of iron.

21. Natives fishing; no success.

22. Our chief out whaling; returned without success.

23. Rainy weather. Natives employed cutting the whale up. Hard times with us, being drove about like dogs; nothing to eat but whale's blubber, which is so disagreeable that we are almost inclined to refuse it, but hunger drives us, and we are obliged to eat it.

24. Clear weather. There is in our chief's house an hundred cwt. of blubber hanging over the place where he sleeps.

25. Our chief out a whaling; returned with no success. Employed cutting fire wood.

26. Employed washing. Natives fishing. P. M. Invited to a feast consisting of whale's blubber.

27. This day one of the natives killed a whale, and he gave to our chief six hundred weight of blubber. I was invited to eat of it.

28. There is such feasting of blubber amongst the natives they eat twenty times a day.

29. Our chief out whaling; natives fishing, &c.

30. This morning the natives were alarmed at hearing two guns fired in the offing, but could see no ship.

May 1. (Monday.) Natives fishing, with no success.

2. Rainy weather. Our chief out whaling ; returned, no success;

3. Fine and clear. Employed washing our clothing. Our chief out whaling ; returned, no success.

4. Our chief whaling. Arrived six canoes from the Wickeninishes with forty bags of herring spawn for our chief.

5. Rainy weather. Employed cutting fire wood ; P. M. returned. Invited to eat blubber.

6. Fine and clear weather. We begin to be very uneasy at not hearing of the arrival of some ship on the coast.

7. (Sunday.) Went to prayers as usual for our release.

8. Rainy weather. Our chief out whaling ; P. M. struck one, but his line parted, and he returned with no success.

9. This day the natives had a meeting at the chief's house to determine what should be done with us in case a ship should arrive. The common natives were always for killing us, but the chiefs would not consent to it.

10. Employed making tompkins for the guns.

11. Fine and clear. Natives fishing. Our chief out whaling ; returned with no success.

12. Rainy weather. Invited to eat dried hallibut. Our chief out whaling ; returned with no success.

13. Fine and clear. This day our chief was informed that three of his captains intended to kill him, of which he informed us ; we were ordered to keep watch over him night and day with a brace of pistols.

14. Natives fishing. This being Sunday went to prayers.

15. This day arrived two canoes from the Wickeninishes with natives who intended to kill our chief, but having had intelligence of it, we were ready to receive them : it was also their intention to have killed Thompson and myself. I will leave it to the reader to judge our situation at this time.

16. This day the natives went home without accomplishing their design. They were frightened at seeing us with a brace of pistols and a cutlass by our side.

17. Natives fishing. We walked all last night before our huts to keep watch, and at twelve o'clock fired one of the great guns off for an alarm, in order to terrify the natives who had left us the day before, and as a signal to them, that we were on our guard.

18. We constantly fire one of the great guns at twelve o'clock in the night and at four in the morning.

19. Thompson employed making a sail for our chief's canoe.

20. This day a whale drove ashore about six miles from Nootka; the natives employed cutting it up and bringing it home in their canoes; the stench of it was very disagreeable, but it does not all affect the natives.

21. This day I am twenty-one years of age. I now begin to give up all hopes of ever seeing a Christian country, or a Christian face, for the season being so far advanced and not hearing of the arrival of any ship on the coast, we feel ourselves very unhappy. We have lived very well during the last week, because our chief was afraid of his life, and had Thompson and myself to guard him night and day. If we could hear of a ship being either to the northward or southward of us, we could dispatch a canoe with a letter, informing of our being in captivity. We are very much cast down at the thought of spending the remainder of our days amongst these savages.

22. Fine and clear weather. Thompson employed making a whaling line for our chief. The summer season sets in very soon. On the 13th instant we eat a pint of ripe brambleberries. Nootka being our Summer quarters till the first of September, when we go to Tasshees, which is situated on the N. E. side of the sound. On the east side the sail is very good for many miles up, low land for ten miles. Cooptee is situated on the same side. Tasshees and Cooptee rivers abound with salmon, herrings, sprats, &c.

23 Employed making a whaling line for our chief; he came into the woods where we were at work and asked us if we were hungry; we told him yes, and he sent us some dried cod fish and train oil.

24. Fine and clear weather. Natives fishing, &c. This day our chief out whaling. Finished the whaling line; took a walk to wash ourselves, forty of the natives threw stones at us, when we asked the reason for so doing, they told us they were only playing.

25. Our chief out whaling; returned, no success.

26. Natives fishing. &c. Chief out whaling; returned, no success.

27. Employed washing clothes, and a blanket for our chief.

28. Natives fishing, &c. Employed cutting fire wood. Our chief out whaling; returned, no success.

29. Natives fishing. Employed making a whaling line for our chief. Natives returned with good success.

30. Employed making harpoons for our chief; he is out whaling. Arrived a canoe from the Wickeninishes with the chief, who came with an intention to purchase me; but our chief would not dispose of me.

31. The whaling season is now over.

June 1, (Wednesday.) Pleasant weather. Natives fishing. Plenty of hallibut and cod fish, which the natives cut up in pieces to dry.

2. Arrived three canoes with dried salmon for our chief. This day we had a dance by our chief's son, to entertain the strangers.

3. Rainy weather. Hungry times with us; nothing to eat but smoked blubber and train oil.

4. Fine weather. This day our chief told us to buy a canoe, fish hooks, &c. and go a fishing, or else he would give us nothing to eat.

5. Employed furnishing ourselves with the necessary utensils for fishing. We were obliged to part with our great coats and other wearing apparel, which used to serve us instead of a bed. Very down hearted, for we are afraid that in a few months we shall be obliged to go naked.

6. Employed putting our fishing implements in order, for fishing tomorrow.

7. This day went a fishing; returned, no success; could not so much as get one bite.

8. Foggy weather. Went a fishing; returned, no success.

9. Clear weather. We went a fishing; returned, no success. Natives fishing, with good success. I told our chief that we did not understand fishing; he then told us to go no more.

10. This morning one of the natives took our canoe without asking us for it, and went a fishing. I informed our chief of it; he told me I must watch for him and when he returned to let him know, which I accordingly did; when the man returned our chief went to him and took all the fish he had caught and gave them to me, told him that he must not take the canoe again without asking leave of us.

11. This day one of the natives killed a sea otter, we had it cooked at our chief's house; it was very good eating. Went to prayers, as usual on Sundays.

12. The natives were engaged in fishing.

13. This day Towtuck, one of the chiefs died. He had been sick ten months, was one of the first that spoke of des-

troying our ship's company, and he killed two of the people that were ashore drawing the scene. Two months after he was struck by the appearance of their apparitions, and during the whole time of his illness he thought they were always in his presence. It gives us great satisfaction to think that God has taken this fellow and two of his children out of existence, which very much terrified all the other natives.

14. Natives fishing; had good success—We were employed in cutting fire wood.

15. We have had nothing to eat at our chief's house for three days. I asked him for something but he told me to go upon the rocks and gather muscles and lampreys, which was a thing almost impracticable, and I was driven to the last necessary means of procuring sustenance to give my handkerchief from off my neck for a dried salmon and a little train oil.

16. Employed in washing our cloaths.

17. This day one of the natives struck a sea otter and brought it to our house. Employed in cutting fire wood.

18. This day being Sunday we went to prayers for our release.

19. The natives take our canoe when they please, if we say any thing to them they tell us we are slaves and ask us where our captain is, making signs that his head was cut off, which grieves us very much.

20. This day there was a meeting at our chief's house of all the natives to determine whether they should kill us when any ship should arrive, but our chief would not consent to it. In the afternoon I bought two axes in order to cut wood with.

21. This day one of the natives shot a wild deer; it was the first I have seen since coming on shore.

22. Went a wooding with empty stomachs having had nothing to eat since yesterday. In the afternoon, our chief gave us some dried hallibut and train oil.

23. Employed in washing our cloaths; this day we used the last of the soap we had saved from the ship, so that we are now obliged to wash our cloaths in urine.

24. This day six canoes arrived from the Wickeninishes with dried herrings and train oil for our chief.

25. Employed cutting fire wood. In the afternoon returned and went to prayers.

26. Employed cutting fire wood. Thompson and myself are the only persons our chief makes do this arduous work.

c

27. This day the strangers went away; our chief gave them muskets, cloth, powder, &c. in return for herring, &c.

28. Cutting firewood. Afternoon, invited to eat fresh salmon; afterwards employed in making fish hooks to sell for provisions.

29. This day I bought some fresh salmon, invited our chief and his wife to eat with us, at which he was well pleased.

30. Employed cutting fire wood and in making fish hooks.

July 1. (Saturday.) Natives were fishing with good success.

2. This day being Sunday, I went to prayers as usual.

3. This day Thompson made a pair of canvass shoes, having no European ones left, which he executed very well.

4. Employed washing our cloathing. Afternoon, was invited to eat fresh salmon; made the natives a present of two fish hooks.

5. Employed cutting fire wood.

6. Employed making fish hooks; arrived a canoe with herring spawn, for our chief; I was invited to eat smoaked blubber.

7. Arrived a canoe from Ai-tiz-arts with five sea otter skins for our chief; in return for which he gave cloth, muskets, &c.

8. Employed cutting fire wood; natives fishing. Returned with plenty of salmon.

9. This day being Sunday we went to prayers for our release.

10. Employed making our chief a whaling line.

11. Arrived a canoe from Wickeninishes with two large canoes as a present for our chief.

12. Cutting fire wood; natives were fishing.

13. Invited to eat seal's blubber.

14. This day finished our chief's whaling line.

15. Natives were engaged in fishing.

16. Arrived four canoes from Caruquates with herring spawn for our chief; there was a large feast of salmon at his house for the strangers, and afterwards a dance by the chief's son.

17. Natives fishing; caught plenty of cod fish.

18. This day arrived two canoes from the Clar-zils which is to the southward of Nootka, about two hundred miles.— The natives brought us no intelligence of any ship but the one laying at the Cheenocks, which we heard of four months ago.

19. This day arrived a canoe from Check-clitz-arts which is about one hundred and fifty miles to the north of us ; the men informed our chief that they had been to war with another tribe and killed one hundred men and women, and that there were ships laying at the northward, which we hope will come to Nootka.

20, Fine and clear weather. We hear both from the north and the south that the natives are massacreing one another for want of cloth, muskets, &c. and our chief expects to be obliged to make war with them as they have threatened him on account of destroying the ship Boston, which they say has injured their trade very much, and that no ship will now come to their ports to trade with them.

21. Natives were fishing, &c.

22. This day arrived a canoe from Wickeninishes with one hundred gallons of train oil. Afternoon, our chief invited the whole of his own tribe to eat dried herring and train oil.

23. This day all the chiefs went about nine miles from Nootka, where the natives go to catch hallibut, and plundered them of all their fish, bringing away with them about ninety large baskets full.

24, 25. Employed cutting fire wood. We now begin to enjoy life much better than heretofore, for we can eat the same provisions as the natives, such as sea cow's blubber, whale's blubber, seal's blubber, porpoise blubber, and in short the oil of those sea animals is a sauce for every thing we eat, even the strawberries and other fruit. But we still think our situation is most miserable, and that we shall have to spend the remainder of our days amongst these savages.

26. This day our chief went on a visit to the Wickeninishes, for the first time these seventeen months. I make no doubt that friendship exists between the two nations.

27. Pleasant weather ; employed cutting fire wood.

28. Our chief returned in very good humour. telling us that the Wickeninishes were very good. This is the tribe that Nootka has been much at enmity with.

29. This day arrived a canoe from the Newcheemass, which is situated about two hundred miles to the north. Our chief was informed there was a ship laying at Suthseat, and that the captain's name was Briggs.

30. We are very much disheartened to think we frequently hear of ships arriving on the coast, and that none will come off Nootka so as to enable us to communicate with them.

31. This day our chief had a meeting with the other chiefs of his tribe to determine whether he should give me a wife, thinking it would be better for me than to live single, and said it was very uncertain when any ship would come to our release.

August 1. (Tuesday.) This month comes in with fine and pleasant weather. Employed making two sails for our chief's canoe.

2. Employed making copper rings as ornaments for the wrists, to enable me to buy my winter stock of provisions.

3. Employed as usual ; natives fishing.

4. Employed making copper rings.

5. Employed washing our cloaths. Afternoon was invited to eat fresh salmon.

6. Invited to a feast consisting of porpoise blubber. Being Sunday I went to prayers.

7. Pleasant weather with a clear sky—employed washing our cloaths. Afternoon, was invited to feast on seal's blubber.

8. Employed making copper rings ; invited to eat porpoise blubber ; was also asked to eat fruit with train oil.

9. Employed making copper rings from bolts which I got out of the ship. I made out very well with them, for one ring I could get three salmon, which enabled me to live well while the copper rings lasted.

10. Natives fishing, &c. Invited to eat whale's blubber.

11. This day I was informed by our chief that the king of the Wickeninishes wanted to buy me, but he told him that he would not part with me, as I should be of service to him when a vessel arrived to inform them of the reason of his cutting off the crew of our ship.

12. Employed making copper rings.

13. Very down hearted, no ship having so much as come within sight since our captivity. Afternoon, went to prayers as usual on Sunday.

14. Employed in making copper rings.

15. This day we were obliged to go three miles and bring wood upon our shoulders or we should get nothing to eat.

16. Employed to bring fire wood ; sat down and eat some green pease, which I accidently found growing wild on the side of the river.

17. This day I was informed in what manner the natives put to death six men belonging to the ship Manchester, Capt.

Brian, of Philadelphia. It was nearly in the following manner :—Eight of the natives held one of them at full length on the ground whilst another crammed his mouth full of stones and rammed them down his throat with a sick. It was a most cruel murder as ever assailed the notice of Christia s, and what rendered its poignancy more shocking was that some of them saw the tortures of the others and knew they were to suffer the same.

18. This day arrived three canoes from the Wickeninishes, but they brought us no intelligence of any other ship, than we had heard of before.

16. Employed in cutting fire wood. The strangers went away.

20. Fine and clear weather. Natives fishing.

21. Was invited to eat blubber.

22. This day the Clar-zarts went away ; by the chief called Makye I sent two letters hoping that they will fall into the hand of some christians.

23. Fine and clear weather ; employed in making copper rings.

24. Our chief and myself were employed in taking the powder out of the kegs and putting it into bags ; I was glad to find no more than five kegs remaining which will soon be expended.

25. This day is Thompson's birth-day, being 40 years of age ; employed in cutting fire wood.

26. Employed washing our cloaths and likewise three blankets for our chief ; was invited to eat dried salmon.

27. Employed in caulking and tarring the long boat.— Being Sunday we went to prayers for our release.

28. Employed making fish hooks ; natives were fishing with good success

29. This day I measured our chief's canoe, which is twenty-four feet six inches by the keel, and forty-six feet from the stem to the stern ; it is the largest I have seen.

30. This day I went with one of the natives a fishing ; returned without success. Arrived 4 canoes from Claz-arts with an intention to buy Thompson and myself, but the chief would not let us go.

31. The other tribe trading with the natives.

September 1. (Friday.) Natives fishing. This day the strangers went away ; I sent a letter by the chief.

2. Employed in cutting fire wood. Invited to eat salmon.

3. This day being Sunday went to prayers as usual.

4. Employed in washing cloaths. Afternoon, launched the long boat in order to go to Tasshees to spend the winter.

5. Employed getting a mast for the boat.

6. Fine and clear weather. Natives fishing. Invited to eat whale's blubber.

7. This day I went from Nootka to Tasshees, where we arrived at four o'clock, P. M. This place abounds with high land.

8. Employed in making our houses, &c.

9. Finished our houses. Afternoon—we had a large feast at our chief's house and a dance by his son.

10. This day our chief bought a wife for me, and told me that I must not refuse her, if I did he would have both Thompson and myself killed. The custom of the natives on their being married is that the man and his wife must not sleep together for ten nights immediately succeeding their marriage. It is very much against my inclination to take one of these heathens for a partner, but it will be for my advantage while I am amongst them, for she has a father who always goes fishing, so that I shall live much better than I have at any time heretofore.

11. Employed making copper rings, &c.

12. Our chief called a meeting concerning Thompson and myself at which we were present. He informed us that we must go naked like themselves otherwise he should put us to death. As life is sweet even to the captive, and as we hoped soon to be released, we thought it best to submit to their will without murmuring, though it was a very grevious thing to us.

13. The natives from the Newcheemass begin to bring dried salmon and dried clams to trade for copper rings, &c.

14. Employed trading with the natives; for one ring I received three salmon. This day arrived a canoe from Ai-tiz-arts with skins.

15. I was employed beating a large copper bolt into rings for our chief; it was extremely hard work as I was obliged to work it cold, having no place to heat it in.

16. Our chief gone to the Ai-tiz-arts to buy ifraw.

17. This day I made sixty rings for our chief's wife, twenty of which she gave me for myself. Afternoon—our chief returned.

18. The natives were employed in making snares to catch salmon. Employed in washing our cloaths. Afternoon—invited to eat seal's blubber.

19. Employed making copper rings.

20. We live a great deal better since I got married, for my wife's father is always fishing. I leave the reader to judge of my feelings at being forced to take an Indian for a wife.

21. Arrived a canoe from the Ai-tiz-arts with ifraw for our chief. Invited to eat porpoise blubber.

22. Employed driving piles down in the river for snares to catch salmon.

23. Invited to eat dried hallibut. Afternoon—arrived a canoe from Cheack-clitz-arts, with ifraw.

24. This day I went 40 miles down the sound to catch salmon and herrings, and returned to Nootka at twelve o'clock at night with no success.

25. Pleasant weather ; natives fishing, &c.

26. Natives employed making snares ; I was engaged in making copper rings. Afternoon—invited to eat porpoise blubber.

27. Rainy weather. Employed making copper rings.— Afternoon—arrived a canoe from Ai-tiz-arts with ifraw for our chief.

28. Natives employed setting their snares to catch salmon.

29. Employed making fish hooks and copper rings to sell.

30. Arrived a canoe from Shoemadeth with a chest of salmon spawn.

October 1. (Sunday) This month generally comes in with rainy weather.

2. This day there was a large feast at the chief's house after which we had a dance by his son.

3. Fine and pleasant weather ; natives fishing.

4. Arrived a canoe from Caruquates with ten bags of herring spawn for our chief.

5. Employed in attending upon some strangers.

6. Employed making copper rings.

7. This day employed cutting fire wood ; we have five miles to fetch it ; P. M. returned. Invited to eat whale's blubber.

8. This being Sunday, went to prayers as usual. Nothing particular has occurred these last two days, during which time I have not had an opportunity to write my Journal, for

our chief has sworn he will destroy it : he always says I am writing about him.

9. Employed as usual. Natives fishing, and getting their winter stock of provisions as fast as possible. Invited to eat blubber.

12. Natives fishing. Invited to eat whale's blubber. Arrived a canoe from Ai-tiz-arts.

13 Natives employed making snares. Invited to eat whale's blubber.

14. Arrived a canoe from New-chee-mass with cloth for our chief: the natives gave us good intelligence respecting a ship having been at their nation very lately ; the chief told me his name was Stautes.

15. Employed making a new road to our chief's house. There was a large feast at his house, consisting of salmon spawn, after the feast, a dance by his son.

16. Natives fishing, &c. Employed making copper rings.

17. For the preservation of my health I go every morning, both in winter and summer, to bathe myself, which has proved very beneficial to me. This day completes twenty months since my captivity amongst these savages.

18. Fine and clear weather. Employed cutting fire wood.

19. Natives fishing, &c. Arrived a canoe with strangers, who brought four skins for our chief.

20. Employed making daggers. Natives fishing ; plenty of salmon.

21. Arrived a canoe from Ai-tiz-arts with ifraw for our chief.

22. Natives fishing. Employed making daggers. The strangers left us. Went to prayers for our release.

23. Went thirty miles fishing for seals ; returned with no success. Our chief out fishing ; caught plenty of salmon.

24. Employed washing our clothes. Invited to eat seal's blubber.

25. Natives fishing. Arrived a canoe from Ai-tiz-arts with dried salmon for our chief.

26. Rainy weather. This day there was a great number of salmon caught ; our chief gave me an hundred as a present.

27. Pleasant weather. Natives fishing. Employed making copper rings.

28. Thunder and lightening, with rain. Out cutting fire wood.

29. Employed as usual. Finished two daggers. Natives fishing, &c. Arrived a canoe from Ai-tiz-arts with herring spawn for our chief.

30. Pleasant weather. Natives fishing, &c. Invited to eat whale's blubber. The strangers went away.

31. Invited to eat porpoise blubber.

November 1. (Wednesday.) This day I went with our chief up the sound whaling; returned with no success. Natives fishing, &c.

2. Went with our chief fishing. The place where we set the snare to catch salmon is a river with a very strong current: I went into the river to set the snare, and the water took me off my feet, and I should certainly have been drowned had not one of the natives come to my assistance.

3. Natives fishing, &c. Invited to a feast of dog fish and cold water.

4. Employed washing our clothing.

5. Rainy weather. Natives fishing; plenty of salmon caught. This being Sunday, went to prayers for our release.

6. Employed making fish hooks. Arrived a canoe from Sarvnah with fresh herring for our chief.

7. Fine and clear weather, with snow on the mountains. Employed cutting fire wood; P. M. returned. Invited to eat blubber.

9. Employed trading with the natives; returned to Nootka with twelve skins. The fishing season is over.

10. The natives employed taking up the fish snares in order to preserve them for next season. Invited to eat seal's blubber.

11. Frosty weather. This day arrived a canoe from the Esquates with twenty fine wild geese.

12. Pleasant weather. We had a feast of wild geese at our chief's house. Employed attending upon the chiefs.

13. Fine weather, with snow on the mountains.

14. Natives fishing for herring; great numbers caught. Employed making copper rings. Invited to eat whale's blubber, smoked.

15. This day the natives began a farce, the same as performed the last year; I found it to be sacrifice offered to their God, for their winter stock of provisions.

16. Natives still performing their farce. Employed ourselves cutting fire wood. Plenty of feasting; the natives eat twenty times a day.

17. Pleasant weather. Natives feasting upon salmon spawn.

18. Rainy weather. Employed making fish hooks. Arrived a canoe from Ai-tiz-arts with a large chest of salmon spawn.

19. Pleasant weather. Natives fishing. This being Sunday, went to prayers for our release.

20. Arrived a canoe from Chee-chu-ate ; brought no news of any ship but what we have had intelligence of before.

21. Frosty weather. Natives fishing. Employed attending upon the strangers. Natives performing their play.

22. The natives fishing for herring; caught a great plenty.

23. Rainy weather, with thunder and lightening ; the wind being very high, several trees were blown down. Natives employed securing their houses.

24. The gales abated. Natives fishing for herring. Employed making copper rings. Invited to eat salmon spawn.

25. Frosty weather. Arrived a canoe from Cla-u-quate with train oil for our chief. Invited the strangers to eat spawn.

26. Clear weather. Natives fishing, &c. Employed cutting fire wood. Invited to eat porpoise blubber.

27. This day during the performance of the play, a boy about twelve years of age had six bayonets run into him, two through his arms, and one through each side, and two through his hips, and thus supported was carried three times round a house being lifted from the ground by the bayonets which were in his flesh : this was to me a shocking sight.

28. Employed making fish hooks.

29. This day the natives finished their play, with a large feast consisting of salmon spawn.

30. Natives fishing, &c. Employed cutting fire wood.

December 1 (Friday.) Frosty weather. Very hard times. All the European clothes being expended, I am obliged to go almost naked like the Indians, with only a kind of garment of a fathom long, made of the bark of trees to defend me from the inclemency of the weather. I have suffered more from the cold this winter than I can possibly express. I am afraid it will injure my constitution and make me very weak and feeble during the remainder of my life.

2. Pleasant weather. Natives fishing. Employed at cutting fire wood. Invited to a feast of dog fish.

3. This day our chief's brother bit off his wife's nose, because she would not let him sleep with her.

4. Employed cutting fire wood. Arrived a canoe from Ai-tiz-arts with ifraw for our chief

5. Rainy weather. Natives fishing. Employed making fish hooks.

6. Pleasant weather. Employed cutting fire wood. Natives fishing.

7. This day the natives caught a great number of herring. Employed making copper rings.

8. This day I was obliged to give our chief the only jacket I had left. Very hard times; being forced to give him our cloaths whenever he thinks fit to ask for them.

9. Frosty weather. Natives fishing. Employed cutting fire wood; P. M. returned. Invited to eat whale's blubber.

10. This being Sunday, went to prayers for our release.

11. Fine and clear weather, with snow on the mountains. Invited to eat salmon spawn.

12. Arrived a canoe from Caruquate with Indians, who came with an intention to buy me, but our chief would not sell me.

13. This day we left Tasshes and went to Cooptee, which is about sixteen miles down the sound, where we arrived at four o'clock, P. M. Employed making houses; the natives removing to Cooptee.

14. Frosty and clear weather. Employed making our houses; in the afternoon finished them. Invited to eat fresh herring.

15. Rainy weather. Employed cutting fire wood.

16. Employed making fish hooks. Invited to a feast consisting of dried cockles and train oil.

17. This day arrived a canoe from Claquate with four slaves for our chief, for which he gave in return muskets, cloth, &c.

18. Rainy weather. Natives fishing. Employed cutting fire wood. Invited to eat salmon spawn.

19. Foggy weather. Natives employed as usual. Invited to eat seal's blubber. Arrived two canoes from Sarvanh, with two chests of spawn.

20. Employed cleaning muskets for one of the chiefs. Invited to eat salmon spawn, dried clams and train oil.

21. Employed making fish hooks. Invited to eat salmon spawn. Arrived a canoe from Sarvanh with herring spawn.

22. Natives fishing, &c. Employed making copper rings. Invited to eat porpoise blubber.

23. Frosty weather. Employed cutting fire wood. Invited to eat.

24. Pleasant weather. Natives fishing. Employed making copper rings. Went to prayers for our release.

25. This day employed washing our garment, which is a fathom of blue cloth; we suffer greatly from the cold weather, having only this small garment to cover our nakedness.

26. Frosty weather. Christmas time in my native country, but a sorrowful time for me. Employed cutting fire wood.

27. This day I went with our chief about twenty miles down the sound, to buy ifraw, with cloth, powder, muskets, &c.

28. Fine and clear weather. Natives fishing; plenty of herring; P. M. we returned. Invited to eat herring.

29. Employed making a large spade to cut whale's fins with. Arrived a canoe from Ai-tiz-arts with ifraw.

30. Fine and clear weather, with snow on the mountains. Invited to eat salmon spawn.

31. Went to prayers as usual.

January 1, 1805. (Monday.) The new year comes in with a fine mild day. Employed cutting fire wood. Invited to eat whale's blubber.

2. Natives fishing. This day I finished our chief's spade, which pleased him very well, and he gave me a fathom of cloth for a garment.

3. This day the natives caught a large number of herring. Employed smoking them.

4. Natives fishing. I was employed making fish hooks. Invited to eat herrings.

5. Natives fishing, &c.

6. Frosty weather. Natives fishing. Employed making copper rings for our chief's wife. She gave me some fresh salmon to eat.

7. Fine and clear weather. Natives fishing. Went to prayers.

8. Rainy weather. This day finished ten rings for our chief; he gave me an old musket, which I cleaned, and sold for forty salmon.

9. Fine and clear weather. Natives fishing. Invited to eat whale's blubber.

10. Frosty weather. This day I was informed that a man belonging to some ship on the coast, was killed while ashore cutting wood, by a tribe a long way to the northward of us.

11. Frosty weather. Natives fishing. Employed making fish hooks. Invited to eat whale's blubber

12. We cannot express how bad our situation is; for the natives look upon us like dogs, and drive us to slavery.

13. Fine and clear weather. Employed as slaves cutting fire wood.

14. This day arrived a canoe from Sarvanh with salmon spawn. This being Sunday went to prayers.

15. This day employed making copper rings. Invited to eat salmon spawn.

16. Blows very hard. Last night about twelve o'clock we were alarmed. All the natives came out of their houses with lighted sticks, beating upon a plank which they held before them, and singing to the moon. I asked them the reason of their singing, and they told me that the moon was swallowed by a cod fish, we looked and saw the moon was eclipsed.

17. Rainy weather. Natives fishing. Invited to eat blubber.

18. Employed making a dagger for our chief. Arrived a canoe from Ai-tiz-arts with ifraw for our chief.

19. Employed as usual. Invited to a feast consisting of blubber.

20. Natives fishing. Employed polishing our chief's dagger; P. M. finished it, with which he was well pleased.

21. Pleasant weather. Natives fishing. Employed cutting fire wood. P. M. Went to prayers for our release.

22. Rainy weather. Natives fishing; plenty of herring caught. Employed cutting fire wood.

23. Pleasant weather. It is very shocking to think what we two poor Christians suffer among these savages.

24. This day invited to a feast consisting of fresh herring roasted. At this feast I saw a man eat seventy-five large herring for his breakfast.

25. Natives fishing. Employed cutting fire wood.

26. Frosty weather. This day arrived a canoe from the Wickeninishes with whale's blubber for our chief.

27. Natives fishing. Employed attending upon the strangers, who had a feast at our chief's house consisting of fresh salmon.

28. Pleasant weather. This day the strangers went away. Went to prayers; we are much dejected at hearing of ships being on the coast, and that not one of them will attempt to release us.

29. Thompson has been sick for four months past; but is now recovering.

30. Natives fishing. Thompson making a sail for our chief's canoe.

D

31. Natives fishing. Employed cutting fire wood. Invited to eat porpoise blubber.

February 1. (Thursday.) Arrived a canoe from the Esquates with whale's blubber for our chief. Strangers invited to a feast of herring spawn.

2. This day our chief went to the Caruquates with an intention to give Thompson to that chief, but he resigned it.

3. Natives fishing, &c.

4. Rainy weather. Employed as slaves. Natives fishing. P. M. Returned; went to prayers as usual.

5. Pleasant weather. Employed at the chiefs' houses, cleaning muskets. P. M. Invited to eat dogfish and water.

6. Fine and clear. Employed making fish hooks. P. M. Arrived a canoe from Ai-tiz-arts, with herring spawn.

7. Blows very hard. Natives employed securing their houses. Invited to eat salmon spawn.

8. Fine and clear. Employed at slavery. P. M. Arrived a canoe from Esquates, with twenty pair of wild geese.

9. Natives fishing. Employed cutting fire wood. P. M. Arrived a canoe from Sarvanh, with herring spawn.

10. Frosty weather. Employed cutting fire wood. We suffer extremely from the cold, being obliged to carry heavy pieces of wood, and the natives will not allow us to wear either shoes or stockings. The bottoms of our feet are cut, and we are very lame.

11. Natives fishing. This being Sunday, went to prayers for our release.

12. Fine and clear weather. Natives fishing. Employed cutting fire wood. Invited to eat whale's blubber.

13. Employed at slavery. P. M. Arrived a canoe with salmon spawn for our chief.

14. Rainy weather. Natives fishing, &c. Employed cutting fire wood.

15. Fine and clear weather. Employed mending the long boat. In a few days we expect to go to Nootka.

16. Rainy weather. Natives fishing. Employed at slavery. P. M. returned; invited to eat raw herring spawn, and cold water.

17. Rainy weather. Which prevents our going to Summer quarters. P. M. Arrived a canoe from Sarvanh with fresh salmon.

18. Natives fishing. P. M. Went to prayers as usual.

19. This being a fine day set out for Nootka. Where we

arrived at 4 o'clock. P. M. Natives employed shifting their quarters.

20. Pleasant weather. Employed making our houses; Arrived a canoe from Esquates with forty pair of wild geese, employed attending upon the strangers.

21. This day we had a large feast at our chief's house, consisting of wild geese, &c.

22. Natives fishing. The strangers went away.

23. This day arrived a canoe from Ai-tiz-arts, with four seals for our chief.

24. This day our chief had a large feast of seal's blubber.

25. Employed making a dagger for one of the chiefs, went to prayers for our release.

26. Natives fishing. Employed cutting fire wood. Invited to eat wild geese.

27. Employed at slavery. Natives fishing. Arrived a canoe from Sarvanh with three seals for our chief.

28. Natives fishing, &c. Employed at slavery.

March 1. (Thursday.) This month comes in with cold blustering weather. Natives employed fishing, &c.

2. Employed cutting fire wood. Invited to eat seal's blubber.

3. Pleasant weather. Arrived a canoe from Ai-tiz-arts with four seals for our chief.

4. This day being Sunday, we went to prayers for our release, which we hope to effect in the course of a few months.

5. Employed making a lance for our chief to lance wales with.

6. Natives fishing; plenty of fresh salmon caught.

7. Employed cutting fire wood; natives fishing; arrived a canoe from Ai-tiz-arts with ifraw.

8. Frosty weather. It is impossible to express the sufferings which we undergo, for the savages take delight in hurting our temper.

9. Pleasant weather. This day we had a large feast at our chief's house; ninety-seven large salmon were boiled in one tub.

10. Employed making a harpoon for our chief.

11. Being Sunday went to prayers for our release.

12. Rainy weather; natives fishing; Thompson employed making a whaling line for our chief.

13. Clear weather; I was employed making harpoons for our chief. Arrived a canoe from Esquates with seals.

14. Employed at slavery.

15. This day I made four harpoons for our chief which much pleased him.

16. This day I was taken very sick, with a pain in my bowels which I presume was occasioned by going naked in the cold.

17. We two poor Christians are in a distressful situation This day one of the slaves died, and he was thrown out of the house as soon as the breath was out of his mouth, which is a custom amongst the natives.

18. Pleasant weather. Natives fishing. This being Sunday, went to prayers for our release.

19. This is the first day, this season, of our chief's going a whaling ; returned with no success.

20. Our chief out whaling ; returned with no success.

21. Being very sick and down hearted, our chief gave me liberty to dispense with the girl that he had forced me to take for a partner, which I did with great satisfaction. Our chief out whaling ; returned with no success.

22. Our chief out whaling ; returned with no success.

23. Natives fishing.

24. Our chief out whaling ; P. M. returned, no success. I am still very weak, and have nothing to take but cold water. Natives fishing, &c.

25. This being Sunday went to prayers. I told our chief that the occasion of my sickness was because he had stripped me of my clothes and made me go naked like the natives, which I was not used to ; he then gave me liberty to wear clothes again.

26. Natives fishing. Our chief out whaling ; returned, no success.

27. Rainy weather. Natives fishing. I begin to get a little better, thank God for it.

28. This day our chief had a meeting concerning Thompson and myself. About twenty of the chiefs wanted to kill my partner, but I told them if they killed him it would be well to kill me likewise. Our chief then told them that they should not hurt him.

29. Rainy weather. Natives fishing, &c.

30. Pleasant weather. Our chief out whaling ; returned, no success.

31. Our chief out whaling ; returned, no success. Arrived a canoe from Sarvanh with herring spawn.

April 1. (Sunday.)   This month comes in with fine and clear weather.   Employed cutting up a new pair of canvass trowsers to ravel out into thread, for the purpose of buying something to eat.

2.   This day the natives employed putting down pine bushes in the salt water for the herring to spawn on.

3.   Natives employed as usual.   I have got my mind at ease once more, thank God.   Invited to eat herring spawn.

4.   Natives employed hauling up the pine bushes with plenty of spawn upon them.

5.   Natives fishing ; returned, plenty of salmon.   Invited to eat spawn.

6.   Employed cutting fire wood.

7.   Our chief out whaling ; returned with no success.   Arrived a canoe from Sarvanh with herring.

8.   Went to prayers for our release.

9.   Our chief out whaling.   Arrived a canoe from Ai-tiz-arts with ifraw for him.

10.   Arrived a canoe from Ahowsarts with a large canoe as a present to our chief.

11.   Employed attending upon the strangers.

12.   Our chief out whaling ; struck one and was fast to him ten hours, when his line parted, and he lost him.

13.   This day the strangers went away.   Invited to eat whale's blubber and dried cockles.

14.   Employed making harpoons for our chief ; he went out whaling ; returned with no success.

15.   Our chief out whaling ; struck two, but his harpoons drawed ; returned in a very bad humour.

16.   This day I finished three harpoons for our chief.   Invited to eat salmon spawn.

17.   Our chief out whaling ; returned, no success.   Arrived a canoe from Ai-tiz-arts with four seals.

18.   Our chief out whaling ; struck one, but there being only one canoe fast to him, it filled, and our chief was drawn into the water, so that he was obliged to cut from him.

19.   Rainy weather.   Natives fishing.   Invited to eat spawn.

20.   Pleasant weather.   Natives fishing.   Our chief out whaling.   Arrived a canoe from Clauquates with train oil for our chief.

21.   Very hard times with us ; we eat only once a day : our meal consists of raw herring spawn and cold water.

22.   Blows a very heavy gale of wind.   Natives employed securing their houses.   Invited to eat seal's blubber.

23. This day arrived a canoe from Sarvanh with the news that a large tree was blown down yesterday which fell upon a house and killed four men.

24. Pleasant weather. Our chief out whaling; returned with no success. Invited to eat herring spawn.

25. Arrived a canoe from Sarvanh with five seals; our chief gave in return a musket.

26. This day one of the natives struck a whale and killed him. He gave to our chief nine hundred weight of the blubber.

27. Our chief out whaling; returned with no success. Invited to eat whale's blubber. There is such feasting amongst the natives whilst they have whale's blubber that they eat twenty times in the course of a day.

28. This day one of our chiefs struck a whale and killed it. This was good news for us, for now we shall live well for some time; the chief invited me to eat of the blubber, because I made the harpoon that killed the whale. He gave to me an hundred weight as a present.

29. This day there was a large feast of whale's blubber at our chief's house, after which his son perfomerd a dance.

30. There is nothing but whale's blubber to eat in the whole village, for the natives are so lazy they will not go a fishing whilst they have any remaining.

May 1, (Tuesday.) Fine and clear weather. Our chief out whaling. Natives making oil to save for their winter stock to eat with dried salmon.

2. Natives boiling blubber to make oil. We live very well, for we boil a piece of blubber and gather young nettles to boil with it.

3. Natives employed as usual. Our chief out whaling; returned, no success.

4. Our chief out whaling; he is very angry because he has had no success this season.

5. Natives fishing. Invited to eat blubber.

6. Our chief out whaling; returned, no success. Went to prayers for our release.

7. There was a large feast at one of the chief's consisting of whale's blubber.

8. This day one of the natives told our chief, that last night he heard a big gun fired, saying it come from a ship. We went in the morning to lock for her, but the weather being foggy, could not see her.

9. Employed making harpoons for our chief.

13. Natives fishing. Nothing occurred these last four days. Went to prayers for our release.

14. This day our chief has given over whaling for this season.

15. Natives fishing, &c. Employed making fish hooks to buy provision with.

16. Natives fishing. Arrived a canoe from Ai-tiz-arts with spawn for our chief.

17. We frequently hear of ships being on the coast, and think it hard that none will come to release us.

18. Natives fishing. Arrived a canoe from Wickeninishes with train oil for our chief.

19. Natives employed driving piles down before our chief's house about seven feet high.

20. Natives employed driving piles down before our chief's house.

21. This day I am twenty-two years of age. Employed at making fish hooks. Invited to eat whale's blubber.

22. Natives fishing, &c. Employed cutting fire wood. Invited to eat cockles.

23. We expect a war every day between our tribe and the Wickeninishes, because there is no ship comes to trade with them.

24. This day our chief told me I must go a shooting.

25. Natives fishing. I was out for shooting seals; returned, no success.

26. Arrived a canoe from Ai-tiz-arts with four seals for our chief.

27. This day our chief had a large feast consisting of seal's blubber. Arrived a canoe from Sarvanh with herring spawn.

28. Natives fishing, &c.

29. Employed attending upon the strangers. Invited to eat blubber.

30. Natives fishing. Arrived a canoe from Esquates with wild geese for our chief.

31. This day arrived a canoe from the Wickeninishes with good news. Our chief was informed there was a ship laying at the Clar-zets, and that the king of that nation had given the captain my letters which I had sent last year, and that it is the captain's intention to come to Nootka sound and release Thompson and myself. This was good news indeed to us.

June 1, (Friday.) This month comes in with fine and pleasant weather. Natives fishing. Arrived a canoe from Sarvanh with spawn.

2. Natives fishing. We entertain hopes of being released in a very short time.

3. Since the news got about that a ship is coming to our release, the natives are very good to us, they do not now ask us to work for them. Went to prayers, hoping that a vessel will soon arrive.

4. Natives fishing, &c. Arrived a canoe from Esquates with six hundred weight of blubber for our chief.

5. Natives fishing. Arrived a canoe from Sarvanh with three seals for our chief.

6. Employed buying all the European cloaths I can procure. Arrived a canoe from Sarvanh with herring spawn.

7. This day our chief had a meeting respecting us, to know whether we were to go away in case a ship should arrive. The common natives were for killing us as soon as a vessel should come in sight. But the chiefs were for letting us go on board.

8. Arrived a canoe from the Wickeninishes with the same information as before ; we are now in hopes of seeing a christian country once more.

9. Natives fishing ; Invited to eat whale's blubber ; arrived a canoe from Esquates with three seals for our chief.

10. Both Thompson and myself are in a good state of health at present, for which we thank our God.

11. We are employed mending our cloaths, arrived a canoe from Clar-ah with forty salmon.

12. Invited to a feast of spawn.

13. Arrived a canoe from Sarvanh with salmon spawn ; there was a large feast consisting of fresh salmon.

14. Fine clear weather ; natives fishing ; plenty of salmon.

15. This day one of our chief's wives ran away from him to her parents, on account of not having plenty to eat.

16. Natives were fishing ; invited to eat dried clams and train oil.

17. Arrived a canoe from Clararzarts with information that when the chief comes to Nootka he will bring a letter for us.

18. This day arrived a canoe from Ai-tiz-arts with seven skins for our chief.

19. Natives fishing ; the strangers went away.

20. Arrived a canoe from Cla-u-quate with train oil for our chief.

21. Rainy weather; natives fishing; was employed in making fish hooks, &c.

22. Arrived a canoe from Check-cliz-aits with the news of six ships being at Newhetty.

23. Employed as usual; natives fishing.

24. This day arrived twenty canoes with one hundred of the natives who had their heads drest with white feathers; they came to buy our chief's neice for a wife to one of their chiefs; she is a girl about twelve years of age; they offered for her thirteen fine skins, forty fathoms of cloth, twenty fathoms of ifraw, twenty muskets, two blankets and two coats, which our chief accepted and gave up his neice. After which they obliged us with a dance and a song; when they had finished, our chief invited them to eat raw spawn and drink cold water; he then had ninety large salmon boiled for them of which they eat as long as they could stand, and then went down upon the beach to play at jumping. Thus ended the wedding.

25. Fine and clear weather; employed washing our cloaths.

26. Our situation would not be so bad if it were not for the high prices the natives ask for their seal skins; for could we purchase four or five skins Thompson could make jackets and trowsers of them, he being a good tailor.

27. Arrived two canoes from the New-chat-laits with ten bags of herring spawn and four of dried cockles.

28. Our chief had a large feast consisting of dried cockles and train oil; the strangers went away

29. Our minds are very uneasy to think that we cannot get our release and there being six ships laying only two hundred miles to the northward of Nootka sound.

30. This day arrived a canoe from Ai-tiz-arts with three skins for our chief. Invited to eat dog flesh.

July 1, (Sunday.) Fine and clear weather. Went to prayer hoping that some good captain would come and release us.

2. This day arrived a canoe from Check-ach-lizaits with the news that a tribe of Indians a great way to the northward of Nootka had attempted to cut off a ship; but the crew being apprehensive of their design prevented it with the loss of ten men. The natives told us that the captain and officers were killed, and that the ship fired upon the village and knocked down their houses. We are very much disheartened, no canoe from Clar-zarts with a letter.

3. This day a canoe set out to the northward with a letter which I hope will fall into some Christian hands.

4. Thompson employed making a sail for a canoe; myself making fish hooks.

5. Arrived a canoe from Esquates with train oil for our chief.

6. This day arrived canoes from Clar-zarts with nine skins, three large baskets of an excellent fruit, called by the natives Quarnosse, and two hundred gallons of train oil.

7. Our chief has now about fifty prime skins. The season is very late to what it was last year, there being but little fruit ripe at this time.

8. Went to prayers for our release.

9. Employed washing our cloathing; invited to eat dried clams and train oil.

10. This day arrived a canoe from the Newchadlates with ifraw for our chief.

11. This day returned the natives by whom I sent a letter a week ago. They returned the letter again and told me they were afraid to give it to a ship.

12. This day I went a fishing with our chief in a canoe, caught four salmon and returned.

13. Employed fishing with our chief; caught five salmon.

14. We are pleased at seeing the chiefs brought so low as to be obliged themselves to go a fishing.

15. Employed as usual; arrived a canoe from Ai-tiz-arts with four skins for our chief.

16. This day I was employed making harpoons for our chief as he expects that there will soon be a ship to release us; he wants a quantity of them made beforehand.

17. Employed making chissels for our chief to make canoes with.

18. Fine and clear weather; natives fishing.

19. This day I was engaged in making chissels as usual. At nine o'clock, A. M. the natives were alarmed at seeing a brig in the offing. Our chief came and told me to leave my work and go with him to look at the brig, I accordingly went and saw her bearing up for Nootka: my heart leapt for joy at the thought of soon getting my liberty. The chief sent off a canoe on board of which I put a letter with information that there was no danger in coming into the cove. The canoe brought me an answer by which I learnt that it was the brig Lydia of Boston, Samuel Hill, commander, and that he was

coming in. He arrived at twelve o'clock and came to anchor, but not running far enough into the cove drifted out again, and stood down the sound to look for anchorage. All the natives endeavoured to persuade our chief not to go on board, for they said that the captain would confine him until Thompson and myself were released. I appeared to be very contented being afraid that the natives would be suspicious of my anxiety to go on board. The brig gave us a salute of three guns, which we returned from the shore. Our chief then came and asked me if he had best go on board, and told me that the whole village had been endeavouring to persuade him not to go, saying that the captain would confine him. I told him to go on board, that the captain would use him well, and he accordingly went, taking with him three prime skins as a present, and a recommendation which he wished me to give him.— When he got on board the captain took him into the cabin, treated him with spiritous liquor and told him that he should not go on shore until the two white men came on board.— Two of the people stood over him with a brace of pistols and and a cutlass ; the brig was standing off and on shore. The captain then sent the canoe with the news that the chief was confined, and that he wished us to come off immediately.— The natives were in very great confusion, crying and running up and down the village, saying that their chief was a slave to the whites, and that I had told the captain in my letter to confine him. But I knew while the chief was kept on board. I should be safe, for that they durst not hurt me on that account. They sent me off in a canoe telling me that the chief must come ashore as soon as I got on board. And I promised them he should. When I got near the brig the natives in the canoe were in doubt about letting me go on board and called out for their chief. But the captain looked over the quarter and told them to come alongside or he would fire at them, for he was determined that I should not go back again. They then put us on board, and the captain was glad to see me, and I of course was very happy at being released. He took me into the cabin and shewed me to our old chief, who appeared to be much pleased at seeing me. There was another chief with him, a fine young man, who had no concern in the taking of our ship. He sat in the cabin to keep our chief company.— After I had acquainted the captain with every particular respecting the capture of the ship Boston, I gave him an account of every thing that was ashore in possession of the chief such as skins, and what was saved from the ship's cargo. The captain made him send for them, and told him he should not on shore until every thing was brought on board.

After the goods were brought off, the chief was released, and the brig immediately took her departure from Nootka.

———————

The Names of the crew of the ship Boston are as follow:

Mr. JOHN SALTER, of Boston, America, *Captain.*

Mr. B. DELOUISA, of Boston, *Chief Mate*

Mr. WILLIAM INGRAHAM, of New York, *Second Mate.*

EDWARD THOMPSON, of Blyth in the North of England, *Boatswain.*

ADAM SIDDLE, of Hull, Yorkshire, *Carpenter.*

PHILIP BROWN, of Cambridge, near Boston, *Joiner.*

JOHN DORTHY, of Scituate, near Boston, *Blacksmith.*

ABRAHAM WATERS, of Philadelphia, *Steward*

FRANCIS DUFFIELD, of Penton, England, *Tailor.*

JOHN WILLSON, (Black) of Virginia, *Cool.*

WILLIAM CALWELL, of Boston.

JOSEPH MINOR, of Newburyport.

JUPITER SENEGAL, (Black)

FRANCIS MARTIN, a Portuguese.

WILLIAM ROBINSON, of Leigh, Scotland

ANDREW KELLY, of Ali,   do

THOMAS WILISON, do   do

ROBERT BURTON, of Isle of Man, England.

JAMES McCLAY, of Dublin, Ireland.

THOMAS PLATTIN, of Blakeny, Norfolk, England.

THOMAS NEWTON, of Hull, Yorkshire, England.

CHARLES BATTS, St. James Deeping, Lincolnshire, England.

PETER ALSTROM, Norway.

SAMUEL WOOD, Glasgow, Scotland.

JOHN HALL, Newcastle, England, *Seamen, all of whom were massacred but me & Thompson.*

JOHN THOMPSON, of Philadelphia, *Sailmaker and Gunner,* and myself are the only persons of the crew who escaped this horrid butchery,   *JOHN RODGERS JEWITT.*

CPSIA information can be obtained
at www.ICGtesting.com
Printed in the USA
BVHW01s2223210618
519722BV00007B/129/P